Esse & Friends
Coloring and Handwriting
Practice Workbook

Girl Friends

Esse & Friends Learning Books

Esse & Friends Coloring and Handwriting Practice WorkBook: Girl Friends
Amercian Spelling

(c) 2019 Esse & Friends Learning Books. All rights reserved.

ISBN: 978-0-6486715-8-9

Also available in UK English Spelling and Hardcover versions.

Dearest Esse,

My darling grand-daughter; you may currently live on the other side of the world but you are always in my thoughts and heart.

Keep being gorgeous, kind, loving, forgiving, fair-minded, honest and curious.

Love it when we get to video chat. Love you always!

Bear hugs and sloppy kisses,

NannaChar

This book belongs to:

_____

Color us in!

Esse

NannaChar

Esse & Friends Learning Books

Hello, I am Annique

Practice writing this name!

Annique

Hello, I am Bubba

Practice writing this name!

Bubba

Hello, I am
Carolyn

Practice writing this name!

Carolyn

Practice writing this name!

Danica

Hello, I am Esse

Practice writing this name!

Esse

Practice writing this name!

Fiona

Hello, I am
Gwen

Practice writing this name!

Gwen

Practice writing this name!

Hermione

Hello, I am Isabella

Practice writing this name!

Isabella

Hello, I am Jessica

Practice writing this name!

Jessica

Hello, I am
Kyra

Practice writing this name!

Kyra

Hello, I am Luna

Practice writing this name!

Luna

Hello, I am Matilda

Practice writing this name!

Matilda

Hello, I am NannaChar

Practice writing this name!

NannaChar

Hello, I am Olivia

Practice writing this name!

Olivia

Hello, I am Poppy

Practice writing this name!

Poppy

Hello, I am Quin

Practice writing this name!

Quin

Hello, I am
Rebecca

Practice writing this name!

Rebecca

Practice writing this name!

Sophie

Hello, I am Tahlia

Practice writing this name!

Tahlia

Hello, I am Ursela

Practice writing this name!

Ursela

Hello, I am Violet

Practice writing this name!

Violet

Hello, I am
Wendy

Practice writing this name!

Wendy

Hello, I am Xuxa

Practice writing this name!

Xuxa

Hello, I am Yvonne

Practice writing this name!

Yvonne

Hello, I am
Zelen

Practice writing this name!

Zelen

Practice writing this name!

Practice writing this name!

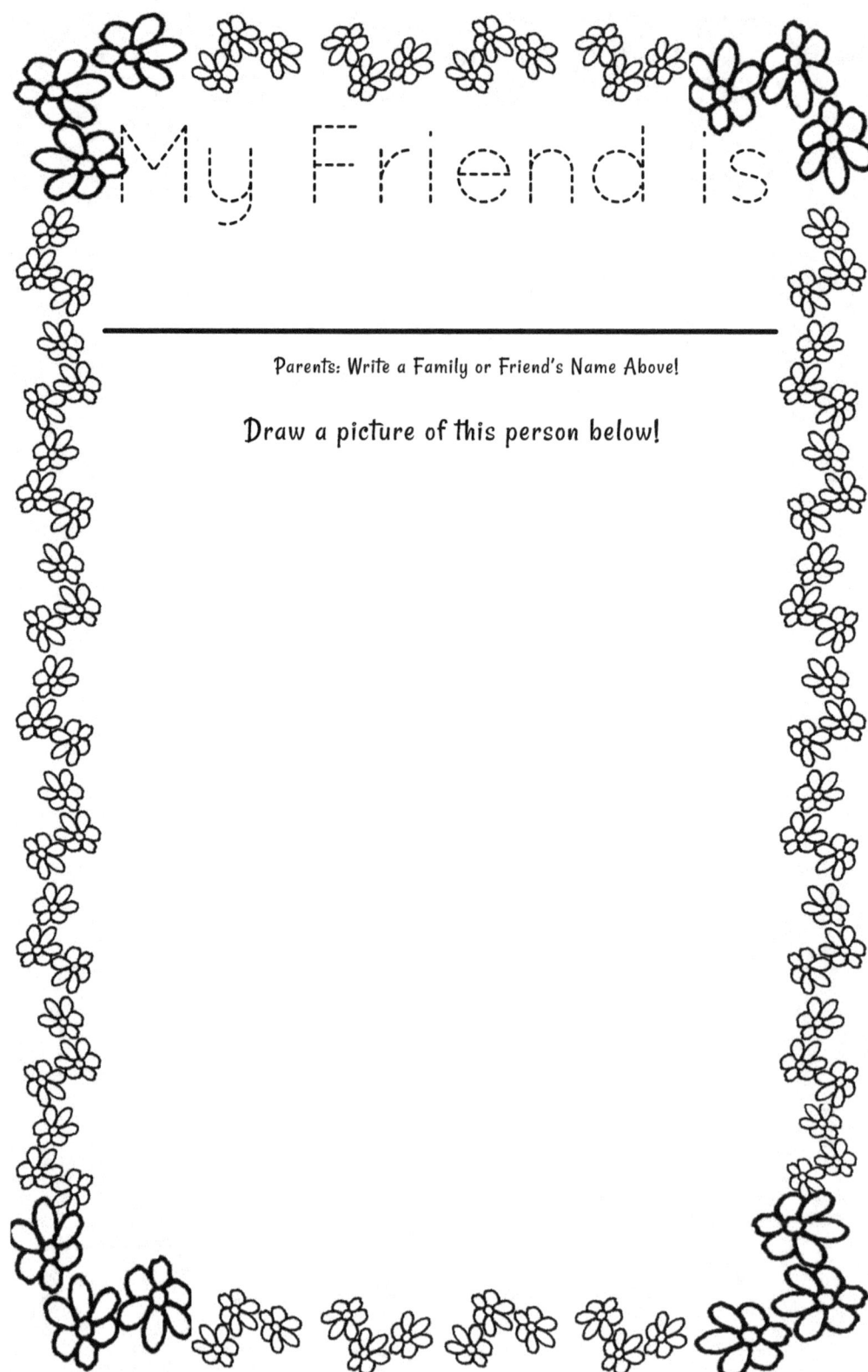

Practice writing this name!

My Friend is

_____

Parents: Write a Family or Friend's Name Above!

Draw a picture of this person below!

Practice writing this name!

Practice writing this name!

Practice writing this name!

Esse & Friends
Learning Books

Attention Parents and Educators!
You are welcome to contact us to enquire about our bulk purchasing discounts and discuss our creating custom words and Esse & Friends interiors.

Be sure to check out the other Coloring and Handwriting Practice Workbooks in this series. Just look for Esse and NannaChar on the cover!

www.ingramcontent.com/pod-product-compliance
Lightning Source LLC
Chambersburg PA
CBHW072108290426
44110CB00014B/1868